THE WEIRD OF GOD: A NEW LITURGY

Edited by Em Ramser

Book Design and Layout by Clent Wyatt

Cover Art by Anna Draussen

ISBN 979-8-9929379-2-3

Midsummer's Lent Books

midsummers-lent.com

THE WEIRD OF GOD: A NEW LITURGY

CLENT ROYE WYATT

POEMS

To all that which may be named God.

CONTENTS

EX NIHILO: AN INVOCATION

There is the void that I am.

I am the void

                                        She hovers over.

                 If I ask—
                 then wait at her feet—
never demanding,
always persistent,

                 She will erect and give shape to

                                what was formless.

From her mouth
She will sing her seed—

                     Her light, filling my darkness,

pushing from within my skin,

                     a crust flaking away,

this passing statue—

                     the graven image of

                                this new giant life

apart from the spent shell of

                     the void that I am.

AT THE CROSS: A HYMN

Others have told me,
if I was the only one,
you still would have hung.
Is this true?
If I was the only one—
would I have crucified you?

I ask for a drink,
you pass me your blood.
I ask for food,
you hand me your body.
I'd rather have truth McNuggets—
quick, easy, and commercially acceptable.

I would live with you in paradise, assurance of blessedness.
You're just so damn insistent on wandering the wilderness.
I would be yours if I could just wear a ring.
You ask too much of me to bear that hateful thing.

At the cross, at the cross—
where the light darkened my sight,
Golgotha collapses both heaven and hell.
God is not but I am
staring back at me.

ASEITY

As I stare into the darkened mirror, I am a body without a head—
only pulsating black space above my shoulders.
Until, patiently, a face shapes itself by pure force of will.

(Have you ever had to reconstitute your self from the ground,
to pull your body back together from the surrounding matter of Earth?)

I coerce this thing I understand to be me to life, away from everything else
I understand not to be me.

Tired of this tug of war—my existence is a fevered dance—around the gravity of
                        some revelatory center that I fear
                                like the fear of God.

Something luminous and monstrous waits to be born
                                        from out this dreaming corpse.
But is it me?
                        I am afraid of not being me.

Let us now minister together, those who have glimpsed this void.
The apophatic God exists in each and for all,
hiding its nothingness in every   chasm   of personhood.
Your shadow speaks to mine and for a moment we are whole
and holy
one in another.

Here we play in our struggles—we learn to play at the slithering heavy abyss
as we learned to play with the feathered aery light.
Nothing will gain us anything.
We are that we are.

HIRAETH

I remember my home—

although, I barely remember a boy
watching the worshipful woods,
basking in the liminal twilight,
and breathing out a prayer for
all the initiatory treasures
(pagan vessels and holy cups)
I buried together
under the bright, disapproving sun—

hoping there they would stay
untarnished,
as the world of me changed
and as my family became simply people—

known, yet strange.

I understand that time is space
and to go back
where a circled cross marks the spot—

the only thing found is homeless memory.

SACRIFICE OR FODDER: AN OFFERING

Must I be thrashed
before the threshold—
my seed, reaped from its husk,
moved beyond
into the siloed temple of holy mysteries
while my rotting straw lies,
left outside the door?

What assurance have I
that I am
in essence the grain
and not the chaff?

What matter is it
if I be consumed
by the walled-off gods or
the penned-in beasts?

Would I not be better served
growing wild and ignorant—
offering myself to all partakers
while remaining rooted and alive?

Yet, then again, I'm dying to know.

MAIDEN AND MESSIAH (AND ME)

The role of the rood, like for Him who came before,
was not tailored for my conception.
It was already there, waiting for someone to take it.

La Pucelle, as Christus was, existed in the beginning—
uttered and fluttered into the wind, a spore-cloud song sung into storm,
looking to fall on just the right listening soil.

The Messiah is to be born in Bethlehem. The Maiden will come from Lorraine.

The violence we would experience for the roles we played
hung in the air, even before our bodies did so.
That we accepted the mantle that would nail us and burn us,
that was the first tragedy—the choice to fit me to it.

Maybe I thought I could use this saintly character more than it using me.
Maybe I wanted to be with Him, my spiritual predecessor.
Or maybe I wanted to be Him.
Our stories were so similar, and I realized at the end it was all too real.
Like me, he was caught up, by choice, by culture, by possibly something deeper,
in a story not fully grasped, a story that stripped us of humanity
and changed us to icon.

I think we both sold and bought the stories of ourselves to ourself
as our own greatest initiates.
A strong personal connection, by nature or nurture,
to the source, found in desert and garden,
that religion only pretends to, by stricture and structure,
fueled our confidence like so much dry wood.
I would have lost my head if I had not burned first.

And once my part was played, the curtain fell—the people, the faith, the divine,
the story—all were done with me, and I was not saved.

I thought he would save me.
So, I was angry with him, the messiah to my maiden,
until I realized he felt the same—
        "My God, my God, why have you forsaken me?"

I am that we are. I got what I wanted, but not in the way I wanted it.

(Listen then to this story, if you are one that feels led by the deeper rhythms—
a peaceful life, lived in obscurity, is greater than all the world's worship of
a martyr's death. Play the part, if you must, but don't forget to bow out before the finish.)

SUPERSTRING THEOLOGY

An ancient Geppetto hangs
between strands of life-lines tied to
carved and lacquered figures caught like
wooden flies in a web.

As their arachnideity articulates,
they animate their limbs
creaking at sinewed joints as
frozen faces flake off in friable color
during this twining dance from the subtle to
the grotesque.

Are they separate or one,
the impetus and the bodies?

Does this threaded God come apart at
the seams in existential dread
with sudden revelation that
the puppets are what make the puppeteer?

I AM! I AM! What am I without them!

LEAVING DUALITY

The Blue Angels, like birds of war soaring
on outspread pinions and brandishing
their beaks and talons, speak to me
with the voice of God—not a merciful one,
but one that wishes to pin me down,
choosing to reduce me to my disembodied faults.

I don't deny my faults,
I don't even deny my faults are part of me.

I deny a god as my authority, who like a bored husband
looking around for some new sexy saint,
now no longer sees why he fell in love with me.

I also hear the hisses of some great subterranean demon,
a waterspout belching up from the earth, its course coiling for a strike.
I've been taught to fear serpents, and for good reason:
one must be an artist skilled in shapes and color palettes to
know which are venomous and which are beneficial.

(Why does my mind make terrible deities and awful monsters from happenstance?)

Now heaven and hell fight over me,
these poor punch puppet players.
Is this my choice—
going back to shack up with the abusive god I know,
or running away with the devil I don't?

It's all sound and fury!

Let these dichotomous signs fade back into the shadows
of a primordial cavern wall and get on with life.

BLAME: A TESTIMONY

God's-Honor, a child of six, died—his head, crushed. I laughed at him, told him to shake it off. It wasn't callousness, I'd just never known death before. It wasn't until I pulled that ballistic monstrosity, that faceless face, away from his own features, and saw the growing crimson pool, his short life soaking into the carpet, that the gravity of the moment soaked into my own crushed mind.

When you turn the TV off, you see yourself.

The instrument of death was a one-eyed idol that never sees but only shows. The eye sat on top, and the body was crafted as a tall metal framework with wheels for feet. It cannot be named evil because like all idols it needed its maker to make it speak and give visions. I provided its force of motion.

When I turn the TV off, I see myself.

My mother, the prophet, always said, "Don't stand so close to the TV." She was right. But who knew it was a statement of physics? The boy jumped onto the monster's body to ride it down the hall—innocence before disaster. Was it my forward momentum in opposition to his downward pull, my life progressing that ended his—a chance meeting or a meeting of fate, bringing two incognizant, antagonistic forces into contact? Either way it's cruel! As it hurled down and he looked up into its face, the TV was off.

I wonder, did God's-Honor see himself?

HAUNTED HOUSE

God's House was my childhood haunt—
a labyrinthine plaything

with dust drenched secret rooms,
dead ends,

and so many ghosts,
both holy and profane.

CHILD'S PLAY: A CONFESSION

As children, we played chutes and ladders.
At church we were taught heaven and hell

and predestination—like the chance of the roll,
I don't get to choose the hanging savior of my soul.

At school I discovered the myth of Prometheus
bringing the light of forbidden fruit,

and finally bored of rigged games,
I set the board aflame.

In the ash, all paths were made the same,
like a snake hung from a pole

for making the sacred the mundane—
one gloriously imperfect whole.

A COPPICE FOR THE HANGED MAN

Weary of looking after that sacred tree,
always fretting about getting it wrong—

(Grow and prune. Grow and prune. Grow and prune.)

I took an axe to the trunk and ended it.

Yet the roots remained.

After years of solace and
letting it lay feral in the field,
when I at last pilgrimaged that way again,
there was no longer one tree but many.
It was an arboreal hydra wearing a verdant crown—

a resurrection to lift up all the hanged men.

TURNING SEASONS: AN ABSOLUTION

I orbit in a spiral of ever tightening circumcision around myself,
cycling between day and night and (from my chthonic view)
moving upwards to an infinite point…

No need to look beyond this body for the resurrection—
I have already lived and lost multiple lives.
Every time I die, a new me rises to take its place—
I pass through this world like the seasons.

You should not fail to let fall the old and dying from the self—
we all change colors—let it now drift away on that sigh.
For anything clung to after autumn will then haunt your ways
as a diminished shade of someone—almost a familiar.

The first lingering will only make the second and third easier.
Soon your life will be devoted to all the stray corpses of you,
rubbing at your ankles and yowling for milk,
and pissing in your house because it's too cold out.

Burn it to ash! Burn it all away!
Lay a Lenten deathbed for spring to bloom.

ASTERION

He holds the center like a burning star.
His kingdom is designed for you to lose your way,
          circles within circles.

Maps are readily available (complicated ideologies)
for the study of supernal geographies.
You can trace your way,
wearing the paper thin and yellowed,
but for an exit they are of no avail—
for always the nucleus pulls
and we, one by one, fall to his lair.

Trampled, chewed, or gored—
the point is you are finally caught in the bullseye.

Those who win are not those who escape (there is no escape),
but those who learn to make a life
amidst the myriad twisting halls.

EZEKIEL 37:1-10, SCRIPTURE FOR BAPTISM

(from The Wet Dream Version)

I can hear the leaves clacking
like a string of seashells in the hot wind—
that oversexed Goddess, born from the dirty pearl foam-spray
of the Gulf, now long gone.

If reality is our perception (if we don't see the world as it is,
but as we are) then do I hear dry leaves or
is it my own sun-bleached bones banging together through bare existence—
an arid purgatory, hoping for rain,
for wet flesh, like a beating animal heart bleating out for love?

I wait for all the stewing tears I've held back to
well up and gargle out, as from a sacred chalice,
to heal the whole wasting world.
I wait for someone else's saliva to mix with my own
in the open krater of my parched mouth.
And life! I am a maid in waiting to actually live a life—
to jump into the fevered river of my veins and be baptized,
overtaken by an ecstatic deluge—
to breathe underwater and drown in shimmering being.

Some protean horse did it once—
may I become a marine-sodden mare,
an ocean within an ocean, a life in life.

IM·MATERIAL: A CALL TO WORSHIP

Hear what I am!
My gaze turned below, I seek to transcend this cold heavenly glow—

to leave behind distant glory (propositional revelation),
and forsake these robes of hoary insubstantial illumination.

From the static infinite to the dynamic here and now—
let me forget gnosis and for one moment avow

the pure awe of being.

Love is lost without sweaty palms and heart beating.

Let me go down where I may live and lust, grow and die.
Wisdom is there in the mundane, not in this airy 'on high.'

THE TAXONOMIST

The worm may die to itself in its cocooned Easter sepulcher,
then at its rapture of resurrection—this entomological Metatron—

I dash away its empyreal hopes and pin it back down among my book of souls,
where I meditate on the importance of structural classification:

three segments, six legs, and wings full of divine significance.
I am the opposite of an iconoclast; once I'm done, the icon is all there is.

AUTHORITY WORSHIPS LOVE, CRUCIFIED

Authority killed love, for love to be a martyr
lying there in our hearts.

Authority feigned love, wearing it as a loose garment,
buying our trust.

Authority hung love on an altar, pointing to it and
averting our eyes from the magician's slight.

Authority now safely reigns, worshipping love as a high hope
while love, with its frozen idol eyes, wantonly watches—
wanting to be taken, brought low and alive.

But authority gained compliance, making love an ideal
dying there in our dreams.

THE PURSUIT

All at once it dawned on me to stop and look around.
What I saw was a great beast
of a machine, of which I was a part,
and my friends and my neighbors,
you too—all apart, all servants of the bloated whole,
so vast it had remained unseen.

There were levels to be sure,
but those above me were still cogs going about their function.
No one visionary had set this in motion;
we all had a hand in writing on the wall
above the door, a single sign:
   the pursuit of happiness.

Yes! That's what we were doing.
But whose happiness?
And what was the definition of happiness—

the whim of a great invisible hand
made of many hands grasping
at the winds for nothing more than icons
from the omnipotent palm of the one.

I dreamed I escaped once, but my dreams are depressingly real
and the truth is I didn't survive long severed from the beast.
I thought maybe I saw people there, just at the edge—
silhouettes against the horizon—
living together outside the paradigm, loving one another.

I smiled as I died,
just as I smiled while daydreaming my death on my own terms
before looking down and resuming my pursuit of a fever-dream that
belonged to no one and everyone.

MIDSUMMER'S LENT

I'm giving up sanity this midsummer.
Like the Baptist, I'm losing my head.

I'm giving up gold this midsummer.
I'll transmute it back into lead.

I'm giving up faith this midsummer.
Perhaps, it's better off dead.

If you look for me this midsummer,
you'll find me aslumber.
I'm letting the heat lull me back to bed.

ACKNOWLEDGMENT: A LAMENTATION

I'm tired of having to learn ways of being,
alien to the life inside.

I want to split open, burst like a seed,
with wails, laughter, and tears—an outpouring.

I want to lash out at this charnel house pantomime of
capital gains and on-brand ideology—a healing wounding.

I want to crucify everything!

If new life rises, so be it.
But assuredly death needs first be acknowledged

as it is already here,
born with us buried in the ground.

FRUITING BODY/CLOTHE THYSELF

A womb knits you into being
from the matter of your mother.
A tomb sows your being back
into the matter of our Mother.
And in between—
we are merely the fruit,
of a greater organism,
hung from that world tree.

Take, eat, this is

/

              their bodies were naked.

I am so transient, like wind animating laundry
hung out to dry,
giving a very specific and rare shape.
Only a moment and I'm gone—the genius of life,
already playing in nearby branches,
has moved on from I.
What meaning does a skirt have?
Patterns, it's all threads and patterns!

PLATO'S REMOVALS

in which a poem is written about a photograph taken of a bridge (or pier) which stood over a pond full of lily-pads and into a wood during fall.

Red, green, and yellow
sprawling out from gray
Dark mirror below
littered with little steps

I mustn't take those steps
They give way to the weight of
it all (or so I'm told)
down, down
into the mirror world

where dark is up and
light is down

My path seems to converge
to a point.

Or is it an illusion?

Is death then a point at
the end of a plane
vanishing
there among shadows

Caught between the
mirror and shadows
my path is clear
What is behind is gone
I could meander, maybe stroll

Yes, I should take my time and
enjoy the colors

at least until the rainy season

I KNOW A SECRET

One must be in the right place
at the right time to see—

the world is full of the spiders' webs
and only the fading light will tell
as you sit, thinking of poems and parables.

Yes, they are woven in the trees between chiaroscuro limbs
but you wouldn't guess in the negative spaces
of the chain-link fence.
And even there, they drape across my window,
forcing this newly framed worldview.

I am fond of the grass between my toes
and of reposing in a meadow,
yet even the back lawn is nothing
but a woven carpet of crystalline filament—
like the vaulted ceiling of the Earth,
strong enough to hold the heavenly bodies.

The leaves of grass are just anchors for the trap,
laid and set—
life feeds life and goes unnoticed.

I don't know if I should now fear
every nook and cranny of

       open

              space

or if I should fall in love with the spider's web.

SQUIRREL HUNTING

First things first. After the triggered cause,
the body falls from up high in its family tree
and hits the earth with a soft sigh of padded leaves.
If you hadn't wished or guessed its fall,
you would have let it lie covered.

But you knew. And now you search for what remains.
With youthful vigor you uncover the essence:
the leathered, furry skin for cool afternoons
and tiny clawed feet for climbing,
allowing for its previous elusiveness.

The lack of blood surprises you—
just a dribble at the corners of the mouth.
You almost expect it to jump to life
and elude you once more, scurrying back up.
(Like you expected with your mother's father and your father's father,
then your forefathers' religion, and next…who knows?)
But the cold eyes, they give it all away.

What's left is to go home and imbibe their life,
making them a part of your own.

BIRD WATCHING

When I watch birds fly,
I catch them in the spiral lens of my crooked wand.
Binoculars are no good—
they only tell close data,
never what the bird means.

When I watch birds fly,
I draw and quarter the sky—
like this drawn and quartered nation—
I feel we've had it coming
a long time.

When I watch birds fly,
I do not listen to their lotus song
so I may hear for any sign,
auspicious or otherwise.

When I watch birds fly,
I wonder where it's all headed.
Is the constant rising and falling pointless,
or is there purpose
in riding the wave-sick wind?

At the end when all comes crashing down,
can there be an inauguration of
a new and better age,
or is it only ever birds of prey
and their prey?

AMERICAN ORPHEUS: A SERMON

Out from the mouths of our children an anthemic dirge is heard:
"Our hopes and dreams are dead, yet we love our dreams to death."

Lyre and lies at the ready, all journey to the land of the Furies
where art and artifice fall onto deaf ears.

We have come to reclaim that which is gone.
For the sake of our soul, we put it all on the line,
and even past that damned line, where hope cannot go.

Our poems and songs, our paints of sunlight and starlight
might calm the rampaging beasts of the earth and open air,
but not here, not those money-green with envy.

Those, mold interred revenants, already given into death
yet still chanting, "buy, sell, buy, sell." They think us the least,
us chasers of quiet sadness and overwhelming beauty.
Us, with silly notions of truth, love, and mystery.

Calls now echo across these burning plains for our heads
on silver platters. Fools! Don't they know, down here our lips
will go on with our siren song beneath the waves.

It's true, we who wake serve apocalypse, dispelling that blind bliss
which shrouds the ignorance of our corpse inheritance.
Mired together in Wild Mother's reckoning, we drink full of
forge-fire memory, as our ancestors drown to the dregs to forget.

Do not look back dear friends! And do not partake of
offered fruits, overripe and sickly sweet—
under here, wormy consumption consumes you.

Us who know we have fallen may yet live again,
and a head in the hand can only be held higher.

FALLING FALLOW: A CALL TO PRAYER

Let us fall fallow.
They didn't care when we cultivated ourselves,
when we trimmed and primmed
to look like something we weren't born to.
We tried being domesticated, we tried being productive.
Now we shall stop trying to please.

So, let your art grow indolent and sleepy.
Our hair will vine out around our resting bodies and
sprout from all the places it's not welcome.
Our skin will dry and crack like a massive outcrop of stone.
We will become primitive and uncouth,
a dark wood given over to losing itself.

But, let civilization beware once we're reborn—
a monster unseen since before we painted on cavern walls.
In that day, our songs will be howls,
our poems will be unformed chants,
in worship of a vast, round goddess giving birth as she devours.
When we wake up, we too will be hungry and horny,
and the city gates will not hold against our rampage.

A FOLIATE HEAD DISGORGES

Raze up!

I stand in the question of stacked stones I did not raise—
this altar is a human ruin where trees pray in rotted pews
and vines lift their tendrilled hands to the sun shining in,
half through colored planes of frozen time and half unadulterated,
the artificial arch of his heaven having long fallen down
to the soil of her Earth.

Raze up!

After my first dumbfounded eternities, my forsaken mouth cracks open
and the cacophony of dusty words that spore out becomes
a ramshackle shed I build, logos by logos,
in order to house myself in that place where grief and awe commingle.

Raze up!

Something's been eating at me,
some nameless wild thing growing up through me
from the snail mucus and mycelium beneath the soles of my feet,
its ancient mysteries branching out around my head—
a hungry haloed thicket of thorns.

Raze up!

Is this where God is?
Not the church, but in what creates the ruin—
the State, the Structure, is what we thought God is—
our ego is what we thought.

Raze up!

Resurrection is Apocalypse—
it came for the Curtain to the Holiest and it comes again now.
Change is sprouting from buried roots to break open our cornerstones.

It will raze up!

Is there to be a beyond for this temple of mine?
Because I am already choking on leaves.

VÖLVA: A COMMUNION

The thrice-faced Goddess
poses still as stone,
prophesying
the singular Sheela na gig.
That wanton witch—

grasping and gaping her mushroom-splayed cup,
unveiling and profaning the holy of holes,
giving out divine secrets as horny tricks and favors,
and birthing all the endless aspects of God
through her soft gargoyle spout—

she lifts that grand proscenium curtain
and begins this mystery play.
Now, what better way to partake and
be born-again
than by the grail of the feminine?

Take, eat, this is Her body.

BRIDAL CHAMBER

I found you at church (a bit more cultish than I remembered)
and I put in my membership to be with you.
A mystery play was performed in my honor
where a fire-haired horse girl,
swinging out her razing-sharp wand to the rhythm of the harvest,
gave a monologue heralding my secret name
(I'll be damned, but you know, I forgot it).

Waiting for the middle act surprise, I was shrouded in a magician's box.
Or was it the Holy of Holies?
I can't recall, but either way it was Death,
the only sure second birth canal, that enveloped me there.

Here the story was still being written, as to whether I stayed dead
or rose back to life, and I began to lose faith along with air
until you snuck in by hidden ways, pressed your mouth to mine,
and claimed me for your own.

As we were intimate, first our genders, then all identity
        mixed.
We watched an orientation on our changing
        bodies,
how we would melt into each other to form a new
        being,
a squat and broad deity wearing its heart on the
        outside.
As one, we would travel the universe by use of our own
        Merkabah,
allowing us to find a disused planet and populate it with our
        imagination.

Reborn, I pushed through the front doors of the temple,
the parking lot now a makeshift launching pad,
all prepared for the me that was us to form a vehicle of light
(as I was now enlightened)
and soar up into the firmament.

But I didn't.
Perhaps I thought the notion silly
and, even though we were one,
I missed you.
So instead, we drove home,
left our contrived purpose on some careless altar, and lived
happily…

ALL SKIN: ANOTHER HYMN

Identity is a skin!
Like frogs we shed
and
devour that gory placenta of what was.

Born again, naked and new,
we testify our true self

in the cleansing rain and thunder

we steal from the gods
the power of death and resurrection.

Identity itself is ours to
dissolve and solidify again
and again
and again
in endless form.

Solve et Coagula—

the mystery of transition,
the power of renewal—

All is Being
and Being is beautiful.

THE WEIRD OF GOD

S   O   U   L   V   E   N   T   freeflowfluid thought-forms,
patterned and patented paternal seed, coming up into motherial being before dissolving
back down, this is our Infinite (w)h0le.

I am a giant, with head in the clouds and feet on the ground, creating on earth
as it is in heaven, singing the singified, the Weird of God and sign of our time,
in the land of the drowned and twice born, where we do not drink (if we can help it)
because we are all and at all times drunk on the all chemical philosopher's solution.

The american life is baptized in anointment and we are the wellspring of that black abyss.
It is the slippery cornerstone of our Bubble (bauble, bauble for which to toil and trouble),
the babeling geneius pool which gives firm to the works of our hands,
a cosmical cauldron of cheap conformts.

It is our leaven and shell, this homogenous material dissolution
(there goes everybody, HydroCarbonEnergy), the flesh returned to the pre-life muck,

the same plaster then interspun into a web to house our Digitus Mundi,
from where all cast images come again to treble our plight.

In this vice-and-virtue-all otherworld humanity is revealed, forever its own Mass
market Eucharist. Behold, the all-gorge-rhythm Ouroboros!
An Anthropos reduction—take, eat, this is our body.
We consummate consumption!

Now what spell(leviathan)bound will we inchant from out the empedoclesean sea of
qwantum potentiality to deceive the SELF? I don't know, but as above so below, life is
found in death. Here! Hold my bronzed sundial sole. I am that I am jumping into the fire,
for an end, a beginning, an eternal return, an apocalyptheosis…

Descent or Ascent (anything but here alive and transient) it's all the same—
soluble s   o   u   l   s sold the salveation s e o n l o u s t k i n o i n h o t f l t l h a e
                                   O   V   E   R

JOHN 17:21-23, SCRIPTURE FOR REVELATION

(from The Mystics' Good News Translation)

Question: What would it feel like to be one with God?
Answer: It would feel like just me.
Conclusion: I am, I am, I am.

Question: What does it mean that I am one with God?
Answer: It means there is no authority over me.
Conclusion: I am free, I am free, I am free.

Question: What does it mean that I am free from God?
Answer: It means I do what I will.
Choice: I choose love, I choose love, I choose love.

GOD DREAMS OF WATERSKINS: A BENEDICTION

We are God, everyone, pretending to be human,
pretending to be fallen.
Drinking from plastic bottles,
we are miles away from our own skins—
        we no longer know our kin.

Their collective animal breath hangs over them,
an exhausted spirit in the hot morning air,
shimmering like an oil spill over the dull disk of light.
        What frightful omen is this?

Did the old world already give up its ghost?
Yet, it still ambles along as a revenant vision.

Must we gouge out our eyes to
finally stake-end this rotting corpse hidden by the christian-capitalist mirage?
        There is no fresh water there to fill our waterskins!

Our fertile sockets now free to gestate a new worldview,
we blindly feel our ways toward each other. Seeing for the first time
the shared essence of being—a fragile light guiding our darkened sight
        from the backs of our psychedelic expanding mind.

In this muddy field of ash and flood, we will cultivate
the decay in our bodies,
        growing brave and compromised new shapes.

The revelation is that the end of days is a collective gospel come true
(bad news really, but one man's trash and all that).
To combat this self-fulfilling apocalypse, we must dream a new way of living.
        We must dream this God-spell together.

I want to acknowledge *The Banyan Review* who first published "I Know a Secret" in their Issue 16: Fall 2023.

I also want to acknowledge Aaron Wyatt, who prophesied the anthemic dirge in "American Orpheus."

I want to remember the short life of Timothy Page, who is God's Honor in "Blame."

I want to thank courtney marie and Spiderweb Salon for giving me a platform to create and perform for the last seven years.

I want to thank all my friends and family who have read over my work and helped me grow as a poet and a person.

I want to thank Kenzie, Aaron, and Ash for believing in me even when I could not.

And on that note of belief, I want to thank God. Because this book of poetry would not exist without their presence, real or imagined (and whatever liminal states where that distinction may blur). And if they indeed are, then my hope is that they are big enough to hold my beliefs, my disbeliefs, and especially my weird beliefs.

Clent Roye Wyatt is an author, poet, performance artist, and stay-at-home dad living in North Texas. He performs locally in Denton with the art collective, Spiderweb Salon. He is the author of *The Book of Gomer: A Love Story of the Sacred Marriage*. And he was chosen as a finalist for *The Banyan Review*'s 2023 Poetry Prize.

Finding himself in a time and place where all things, even people, are commodified and branded, Clent seeks to infuse his work with a sense of the sacred and the mythic.

ONE LAST WORD: A PROTEST

Where is that rolling river of justice?
Where are they with all things held common?
Where is the one with nowhere to lay their head,
shepherd and lamb, who feeds the masses their bread?
The curtain is long gone, but now a gilded wall excludes instead.

Why do you seek the good among the spiritually dead,
sitting there with the rich and powerful?
At the cross, the lesson is
God dwells in the poor and sorrowful.

But you glance over scriptures, ancient words on the page,
as you wait out coward lives lived strange.
Waiting, waiting, waiting to die
for an afterlife, a good reward,
as if you didn't already chase here
your posessions, your piece of the pie.

I know why you hide and wait.
Because you understand to bring the people inside your gate
(the ones your supposed savior actually lived among),
will cause you to change—
to be disempowered and hung.

Resurrection is preceded by Crucifixion!

But the religious life is too damned comfortable to
be bothered with opposing systems of oppression
or living out communal compassion.
That is not profitable or compatible
with your saccharine platitudes and power fixation.

Worldly strength and false peace are what Satan offered,
and now that it is still proffered
you accept it with abandon.
There is no Christ in your communion,
only a demonic feast
as you sit at the feet of the beast.
And gnawing on the least of these,
you intoxicate yourself on the fruit of your iniquities.

There is no washing your hands of this—
it is written on your foreheads.
Truth has fled from you
and the whole world sees.

Woe to the Church in America!
Woe to your privileged and prideful misdeeds.
Woe to your bigotry and lack of empathy.
Woe to your hollow and harmful creeds.
The seeds have been planted.
You reap what you sow.
Your curses now breed.
Watch them turn to your woe, woe, woe.